Robertson

by Iain Gray

PUBLISHING

WRITING *to* REMEMBER

79 Main Street, Newtongrange,
Midlothian EH22 4NA
Tel: 0131 344 0414
E-mail: info@lang-syne.co.uk
www.langsyneshop.co.uk

Design by Dorothy Meikle
Printed by Printwell Ltd
© Lang Syne Publishers Ltd 2024

All rights reserved. No part of this publication may be reproduced, stored or introduced into a retrieval system, or transmitted in any form or by any means (electronic, mechanical, photocopying, recording or otherwise) without the prior written permission of Lang Syne Publishers Ltd.

ISBN 978-1-85217-643-3

Robertson

MOTTO:
Glory is the reward of valour.

CREST:
A hand holding an imperial crown.

NAME variations include:
　　Robb
　　Robbie
　　Robson

Chapter one:

The origins of popular surnames

by George Forbes and Iain Gray

If you don't know where you came from, you won't know where you're going **is a frequently quoted observation and one that has a particular resonance today when there has been a marked upsurge in interest in genealogy, with increasing numbers of people curious to trace their family roots.**

Main sources for genealogical research include census returns and official records of births, marriages and deaths – and the key to unlocking the detail they contain is obviously a family surname, one that has been 'inherited' and passed from generation to generation.

No matter our station in life, we all have a surname – but it was not until about the middle of the fourteenth century that the practice of being identified by a particular surname became commonly established throughout the British Isles.

Previous to this, it was normal for a person to be identified through the use of only a forename.

But as population gradually increased and there were many more people with the same forename, surnames were adopted to distinguish one person, or community, from another.

Many common English surnames are patronymic in origin, meaning they stem from the forename of one's father – with 'Johnson,' for example, indicating 'son of John.'

It was the Normans, in the wake of their eleventh century conquest of Anglo-Saxon England, a pivotal moment in the nation's history, who first brought surnames into usage – although it was a gradual process.

For the Normans, these were names initially based on the title of their estates, local villages and chateaux in France to distinguish and identify these landholdings.

Such grand descriptions also helped enhance the prestige of these warlords and generally glorify their lofty positions high above the humble serfs slaving away below in the pecking order who had only single names, often with Biblical connotations as in Pierre and Jacques.

The only descriptive distinctions among the peasantry concerned their occupations, like 'Pierre the swineherd' or 'Jacques the ferryman.'

Roots of surnames that came into usage in England not only included Norman-French, but also Old French, Old Norse, Old English, Middle English, German, Latin, Greek, Hebrew and the Gaelic languages of the Celts.

The Normans themselves were originally Vikings, or 'Northmen', who raided, colonised and eventually settled down around the French coastline.

They had sailed up the Seine in their longboats in 900AD under their ferocious leader Rollo and ruled the roost in north eastern France before sailing over to conquer England in 1066 under Duke William of Normandy – better known to posterity as William the Conqueror, or King William I of England.

Granted lands in the newly-conquered England, some of their descendants later acquired territories in Wales, Scotland and Ireland – taking not only their own surnames, but also the practice of adopting a surname, with them.

But it was in England where Norman rule and custom first impacted, particularly in relation to the adoption of surnames.

This is reflected in the famous *Domesday Book*, a massive survey of much of England and Wales, ordered by William I, to determine who owned what, what it was worth and therefore how much they were liable to pay in taxes to the voracious Royal Exchequer.

Completed in 1086 and now held in the National Archives in Kew, London, 'Domesday' was an Old English word meaning 'Day of Judgement.'

This was because, in the words of one contemporary chronicler, "its decisions, like those of the Last Judgement, are unalterable."

It had been a requirement of all those English landholders – from the richest to the poorest – that they identify themselves for the purposes of the survey and for future reference by means of a surname.

This is why the *Domesday Book*, although written in Latin as was the practice for several centuries with both civic and ecclesiastical records, is an invaluable source for the early appearance of a wide range of English surnames.

Several of these names were coined in connection with occupations.

These include Baker and Smith, while Cooks, Chamberlains, Constables and Porters were to be found carrying out duties in large medieval households.

The church's influence can be found in names such as Bishop, Friar and Monk while the popular name of Bennett derives from the late fifth to mid-sixth century Saint Benedict, founder of the Benedictine order of monks.

The early medical profession is represented by Barber, while businessmen produced names that include Merchant and Sellers.

Down at the village watermill, the names that cropped up included Millar/Miller, Walker and Fuller, while other self-explanatory trades included Cooper, Tailor, Mason and Wright.

Even the scenery was utilised as in Moor, Hill, Wood and Forrest – while the hunt and the chase supplied names that include Hunter, Falconer, Fowler and Fox.

Colours are also a source of popular surnames, as in Black, Brown, Gray/Grey, Green and White, and would have denoted the colour of the clothing the person habitually wore or, apart from the obvious exception of 'Green', one's hair colouring or even complexion.

The surname Red developed into Reid, while

Blue was rare and no-one wanted to be associated with yellow.

Rather self-important individuals took surnames that include Goodman and Wiseman, while physical attributes crept into surnames such as Small and Little.

Many families proudly boast the heraldic device known as a Coat of Arms, as featured on our front cover.

The central motif of the Coat of Arms would originally have been what was borne on the shield of a warrior to distinguish himself from others on the battlefield.

Not featured on the Coat of Arms, but highlighted on page three, is the family motto and related crest – with the latter frequently different from the central motif.

Adding further variety to the rich cultural heritage that is represented by surnames is the appearance in recent times in lists of the 100 most common names found in England of ones that include Khan, Patel and Singh – names that have proud roots in the vast sub-continent of India.

Echoes of a far distant past can still be found in our surnames and they can be borne with pride in commemoration of our forebears.

Chapter two:

Invasion and conquest

Although a name that is particularly identified with Scotland, where it is ranked 5th in some lists of the 100 most common surnames found there, in lists for England 'Robertson' is also ranked highly, at 27th out of 100.

The reason for the high preponderance of the name throughout the British Isles lies in the fact that it stems from what for centuries has been the popular forename 'Robert', with 'Robertson' indicating 'son of Robert.' The given name 'Robert' in turn derives from the Anglo-Saxon 'hrothi' and 'berhta', meaning 'fame-bright'.

This means that, despite being popularised as a surname in the wake of the Norman Conquest, flowing through the veins of Robertsons today may well be the blood of those Germanic tribes who invaded and first settled in the south and east of the island of Britain from about the early fifth century.

Known as the Anglo-Saxons, they were composed of the Jutes, from the area of the Jutland Peninsula in modern Denmark, the Saxons from

Lower Saxony, in modern Germany and the Angles from the Angeln area of Germany.

It was the Angles who gave the name 'Engla land', or 'Aengla land' – better known as 'England.'

They held sway in what became England from approximately 550 to 1066, with the main kingdoms those of Sussex, Wessex, Northumbria, Mercia, Kent, East Anglia and Essex.

Whoever controlled the most powerful of these kingdoms was tacitly recognised as overall 'king' – one of the most noted being Alfred the Great, King of Wessex from 871 to 899.

It was during his reign that the famous *Anglo-Saxon Chronicle* was compiled – an invaluable source of Anglo-Saxon history – while Alfred was designated in early documents as *Rex Anglorum Saxonum*, King of the English Saxons.

Through the Anglo-Saxons, the language known as Old English developed, later transforming from the eleventh century into Middle English – sources from which popular English surnames of today, such as Robertson, derive.

The Anglo-Saxons meanwhile, had usurped the power of the indigenous Britons – who referred to them as 'Saeson' or 'Saxones.' It is from this that the

Scottish-Gaelic term for 'English people' of 'Sasannach' derives, the Irish- Gaelic 'Sasanach' and the Welsh 'Saeson.'

We learn from the *Anglo-Saxon Chronicle* how the religion of the early Anglo-Saxons was one that pre-dated the establishment of Christianity in the British Isles. Known as a form of Germanic paganism, with roots in Old Norse religion, it shared much in common with the Druidic 'nature-worshipping' religion of the indigenous Britons.

It was in the closing years of the sixth century that Christianity began to take a hold in Britain, while by approximately 690 it had become the 'established' religion of Anglo-Saxon England.

The first serious shock to Anglo-Saxon control came in 789 in the form of sinister black-sailed Viking ships that appeared over the horizon off the island monastery of Lindisfarne, in the northeast of the country. Lindisfarne was sacked in an orgy of violence and plunder, setting the scene for what would be many more terrifying raids on the coastline of not only England, but also Ireland and Scotland.

But the Vikings, or 'Northmen', in common with the Anglo-Saxons of earlier times, were raiders who eventually stayed – establishing, for example, what became Jorvik, or York, and the trading port of Dublin, in Ireland. Through intermarriage, the bloodlines of the Anglo-Saxons also became infused with that of the Vikings.

But there would be another infusion of the blood of the 'Northmen' in the wake of the Norman Conquest of 1066 – a key event in English history that sounded the death knell of Anglo-Saxon supremacy.

By this date, England had become a nation with several powerful competitors to the throne.

In what were extremely complex family, political and military machinations, the king was Harold II, who had succeeded to the throne following the death of Edward the Confessor.

But his right to the throne was contested by two powerful competitors – his brother-in-law King Harold Hardrada of Norway, in alliance with Tostig, Harold II's brother, and Duke William II of Normandy.

In what has become known as The Year of Three Battles, Hardrada invaded England and gained victory over the English king on September 20 at the battle of Fulford, in Yorkshire.

Five days later, however, Harold II decisively defeated his brother-in-law and brother at the battle of Stamford Bridge.

But he had little time to celebrate his victory, having to immediately march south from Yorkshire to encounter a mighty invasion force led by Duke William that had landed at Hastings, in East Sussex.

Harold's battle-hardened but exhausted force of Anglo-Saxon soldiers confronted the Normans on October 14, drawing up a strong defensive position at the top of Senlac Hill, and building a shield wall to repel William's cavalry and infantry.

The Normans suffered heavy losses, but through a combination of the deadly skill of their archers and the ferocious determination of their cavalry they eventually won the day.

Morale had collapsed on the battlefield as word spread through the ranks that Harold, the last of the Anglo-Saxon kings, had been killed.

William was declared King of England on December 25, and the complete subjugation of his Anglo-Saxon subjects followed.

Those Normans who had fought on his behalf were rewarded with the lands of Anglo-Saxons, many of whom sought exile abroad as mercenaries.

Within an astonishingly short space of time, Norman manners, customs and law were imposed on

England – laying the basis for what subsequently became established 'English' custom and practice.

But beneath the surface, old Anglo-Saxon culture was not totally eradicated, with some aspects absorbed into that of the Normans, while faint echoes of the Anglo-Saxon past is still seen today in the form of popular surnames such as Robertson.

The popularity of the name meant that its bearers came to be found all over England, although the first recorded spelling – in the form of 'Robertsone' – appears in Derbyshire in 1327, and it is with this modern-day English county that it is particularly identified.

In Scotland, some bearers of the name today may be entitled to trace a descent, in common with some English bearers of the name who can identify a Scottish ancestry, from the proud Clan Robertson who in turn trace a descent from ancient Celtic Earls of Atholl.

Also known as Clan Donnachaidh, from 'Duncan', the clan adopted 'Robertson' as a surname from Robert, 4th Chief of the Clan.

Bearers of the name came to feature prominently in the historical record through a range of endeavours and pursuits.

In the ecclesiastical realms, The Right Reverend George Samuel Robertson was the noted Bishop of Exeter born in 1835 in Sywell, Northamptonshire. Graduating with a first class degree in classics from Trinity College, Oxford, he served as Principal of King's College, London from 1897 to 1903 when he was appointed Bishop of Exeter.

Serving as bishop until 1916, he died in 1931, while his father, Archibald Robertson, had been the Scottish physician, ship's surgeon and medical writer born in 1789 in Cockburnspath, Berwickshire.

Present in 1809 on the Royal Navy flagship *Caledonia* when the British naval commander Lord Dundonald attempted to burn the French fleet in Basque roads, in 1818 he established a medical practice in Northampton and wrote a number of medical treatise.

A Fellow of the scientific think-tank the Royal Society and also a member of the Royal Society of Edinburgh, he died in 1864.

Chapter three:

Battle honours

Bearers of the Robertson name have gained particular distinction on the bloody field of battle.

Born in Dumfries in 1865, William Robertson was a Scottish recipient of the Victoria Cross (VC), the highest award for valour in the face of enemy action for British and Commonwealth forces.

He had been a sergeant-major in the 2nd Battalion, The Gordon Highlanders, during the Second Boer War, when in October of 1899 at the battle of Elandslaagte he braved withering enemy fire to lead a successful assault on a position and, despite being wounded, to hold it until relieved.

Promoted to captain in 1910, major in 1915 and lieutenant-colonel in 1917, he was appointed honorary treasurer of the Royal British Legion Scotland following his retirement from the army in 1920.

The recipient of a CBE, he died in 1949, while his VC is now on display at the National War Museum of Scotland, Edinburgh Castle.

Born in 1883 in Pictou County, Nova Scotia,

James Robertson was a posthumous recipient of the VC during the First World War.

He had been a private in the 27th (City of Winnipeg) Battalion, Canadian Expeditionary Force when, in November of 1917 during the final assault on Passchendaele, in Belgium, he was killed by a bursting shell after having not only single-handedly killed an enemy machine-gun crew but also rescuing a wounded comrade.

Also during the First World War, William Robertson, later 1st Baronet of Welbourn, Lincolnshire is, to date, the first and only British Army soldier to rise from the rank of private to Field Marshall.

Born in 1860, he enlisted in the army in 1877 and served for twelve years as a trooper in the 16th (The Queen's) Lancers, while in 1897 he was selected to attend the Staff College, Camberley.

His subsequent rise through the army establishment was rapid, serving from 1916 to 1918 as Chief of the Imperial Staff (CIGS); also known fondly as "Wully" Robertson, he died in 1933.

His son General Brian Hubert Robertson, born in 1896 and later 1st Baron Robertson of Oakridge, also served during the First World War and went on to hold posts that included, following the end of the Second World War, Military Governor and British member of the Allied Control Council for Germany.

Chairman from 1953 to 1961 of the British Transport Commission, he died in 1974.

In the smoke and mirrors that is the world of deception, Thomas Argyll Robertson, born in 1909 and known as "Tommy" or more commonly by his initials 'TAR' was the British military intelligence officer responsible for the disinformation campaign against the Germans known as *Double Cross*.

In addition to 'turning' captured German spies to feed disinformation back to the Abwehr, German military intelligence, and also to persuade German High Command that the planned invasion of Hitler's *Festung Europa* – Fortress Europe – would take place at the Pas de Calais, and not Normandy, *Double Cross* also involved the complex but ultimately successful *Operation Mincemeat*.

This was to persuade the Germans that the Allies planned to invade Greece and Sardinia in 1943 – and not Sicily as was actually planned through what was known as *Operation Husky*.

A scheme was devised by Robertson and what was known as the *XX-Committee* – a team that included the Royal Navy intelligence officer Lieutenant Ewen Montagu – to arrange for the body of a British officer, carrying apparently top secret documents revealing the Allies planned to invade Greece and Sardinia, to be washed up on a beach in Punta Umbria, Spain.

The planners were aware the Spanish authorities, although ostensibly neutral, regularly co-operated with the Abwehr and would pass on for its examination any documents found on the body.

Accordingly the body of a man who had died in London from symptoms that closely resembled hypothermia and drowning was obtained from a coroner.

It was not until many years later that it was revealed he was Glyndwr Michael, a 34-year-old Welshman who had no living relatives.

A 'legend' was created that the corpse was that of Captain (Acting Major) William "Bill" Martin of the Royal Marines and, in addition to the 'top secret' military documents, love letters and even a bill from a jeweller for an engagement ring for his fiancée were planted on him.

The body was floated out to sea to wash up on the beach at Porta Umbria and the authorities, as hoped, passed all the documentation and Martin's personal possessions on to the Abwehr for their examination.

The Abwehr fell for the ruse and accordingly German High Command depleted its forces in Sicily in favour of Greece and Sardinia – contributing in no small measure to the success of *Operation Husky*.

The story was used as the plot of a 1950 novel, *Operation Heartbreak*, by Duff Cooper, who had held a number of wartime posts – but three years later the true tale of *Operation Mincemeat* was revealed by Lieutenant Commander Montagu in *The Man Who Never Was*, adapted for a film of the name in 1956.

Robertson, the recipient of an OBE for his clandestine wartime service, died in 1994, while after the war Winston Churchill had written: "In wartime, truth is so precious that she should always be attended by a bodyguard of lies."

Going back to the nineteenth century, James Robertson is recognised as having been one of the first war photographers.

Born in Middlesex in 1813, he trained as a coin and gem engraver, and it was while later working as an engraver at the Imperial Ottoman Mint in

Constantinople, now the Turkish capital of Istanbul, that he became interested in photography.

Along with fellow British photographer Felix Beato, he formed the photographic partnership Robertson and Beato, opening a studio in Constantinople and later joined by Beato's brother Antonio.

Robertson and Felix Beato travelled to Balaclava in 1855 during the Crimean War and, in September of that year, recorded on film the fall of Russian-held Sevastopol to the British and their allies.

Robertson died in 1888, his photographic partnership having produced – in addition to war images – stunning panoramas of far-flung places such as India, Malta, Greece, Egypt and Jerusalem.

From the battlefield to politics, George Robertson, more formally known as George Islay MacNeill Robertson, Baron Robertson of Port Ellen, is the British Labour Party politician who served from October of 1999 until January of 2004 as General Secretary of the North Atlantic Treaty Organisation (NATO).

Born in 1946 in Port Ellen, Isle of Islay, after having studied economics at Queen's College, Dundee, he first entered the House of Commons in

1978 after winning a by-election in the Scottish constituency of Hamilton, later Hamilton South.

His by-election win came just a year after a serious road accident when the car he was driving was involved in a collision with a Royal Navy Land Rover carrying gelignite and a box of detonators.

Fortunately, the gelignite did not explode, but he was left with a broken jaw and smashed knees.

His many political posts have included, from 1997 to 1999, Defence Secretary, while he was also a leading figure in the successful campaign to ban handguns in the United Kingdom.

This followed the murder in 1996 of sixteen children and their teacher at their school in Dunblane – the Scottish town where Robertson lived with his family – by a deranged local man, Thomas Hamilton.

His many honours include honorary doctorates from a number of universities, while in 2003 he was a recipient of America's Presidential Medal of Freedom.

One particularly controversial bearer of the Robertson name is the American media mogul, former Southern Baptist minister, supporter of conservative Christian values and author Marian Gordon Robertson, better known as Pat Robertson.

Born in 1930 in Lexington, Virginia, a son of Absalom Willis Robertson, the Democratic Party politician who represented Virginia in the U.S. Senate from 1946 to 1966, he is the founder of a number of corporations and organisations.

These include the Christian Broadcasting Network (CBN), ABC Family Channel, Operation Blessing International Relief and Development Corporation and Regent University in Virginia.

Unsuccessful in his bid to become the Republican Party nominee in the 1988 presidential election, he is the author of the best-selling *The New World Order* – which has been heavily criticised because of his theory of a worldwide Jewish conspiracy and his castigation of homosexuality.

In 1999, the Bank of Scotland entered into a joint venture with him to provide financial services in the United States – but the bank pulled out of the venture because of widespread condemnation throughout the U.K. of Robertson's views on homosexuality.

His son Gordon Perry Robertson, born in 1958 and chief executive officer of CBN, is a frequent co-host of his father's live weekdays' Christian news and television programme *The 700 Club*.

Chapter four:
On the world stage

Born in 1923 in La Jolla, California, Clifford Parker Robertson III was the veteran American actor better known as Cliff Robertson.

Serving during the Second World War in the United States Merchant Marine and later working for a short period as a journalist, the lure of the stage beckoned and his first screen role was in the 1950 film *Mr Roberts*.

But it was not until thirteen years later that his big break came – when he was personally chosen by President John F. Kennedy to portray him in the film *PT 109*, chronicling Kennedy's experiences during the Second World War as commander of a torpedo-armed fast attack craft designated as a PT (Patrol Torpedo) boat.

Other major screen credits include the 1963 *633 Squadron*, the 1968 *Charly* – for which he won an Academy Award for Best Actor for his portrayal of a mentally disabled man – and the 1991 *Wild Hearts Can't Be Broken*.

Towards the end of his acting career, he came

to the attention of a new generation of film-goers through his role of Uncle Ben Parker in the 2002 *Spider-Man* and two of its sequels,

Away from the stage, his passion was flying and his impressive collection of aircraft included a Messerschmitt Bf 108 and a Supermarine Spitfire.

On the morning of September 11, 2001 – a date better known simply as '9/11', he was piloting his Beechcraft Baron aircraft in the skies above New York's World Trade Center when the first tower was struck by a hijacked Boeing passenger aircraft.

The recipient of honours and awards that include a star on the Hollywood Walk of Fame and induction into the National Aviation Hall of Fame, he died in 2011.

Proudly using 'Robertson' as part of his surname, James Norval Harald Robinson Justice was the British character actor better known as **James Robertson Justice**, sometimes also credited on film as James Robertson-Justice or James R. Justice.

Born in 1907 in Lewisham, London, the rather larger than life actor was the son of an Aberdeen-born geologist and throughout his life he remained proud of his Scottish roots – to the extent that he was sometimes referred to as 'the English Scotsman.'

Studying both science and geology for a time but never completing the courses, he had a natural flair for languages and could converse fluently in a range that included French, Greek, Russian, German and Scots-Gaelic.

Becoming a journalist in London in 1927 with Reuter's news agency, it was not long before the restless future actor left British shores for Canada – where he worked, variously, as a lumberjack, insurance salesman, teacher of English and as a gold miner.

Returning to Britain in the 1930s, the sports-loving Robertson Justice served for a time as secretary of the British Ice Hockey Association, managing the national team at the 1932 European Championships in Berlin.

Fighting on the Republican side during the Spanish Civil War, it was then that he grew what became his 'trademark' bushy beard giving rise to the subsequent nickname in Scottish-Gaelic of *Seamus Mor na Feusaig* – 'Big James with the Beard.'

Serving with the Royal Naval Volunteer Reserve during the Second World War until wounded by shrapnel in 1943, his acting debut came a year later in the film *For Those in Peril*.

But it was for his role during the 1950s and 1960s as the irascible and domineering Sir Lancelot Spratt in the *Doctor* series of comedy films – beginning with the 1954 *Doctor in the House* – that he became best known.

Other film credits – in which he co-starred with Gregory Peck – are the 1951 *Captain Horatio Hornblower, R. N.*, the 1956 *Moby Dick* and, from 1961, *The Guns of Navarone*, which he also narrated.

It was shortly after completing the 1968 *Chitty Chitty Bang* that he suffered a severe stroke that put an end to his acting career.

Away from acting, he had unsuccessfully contested the Scottish constituency of North Angus and Mearns for the Labour Party in 1950, while from 1957 to 1960 and again from 1963 to 1966, he served as Rector of Glasgow University.

Married twice, he died penniless in 1975 and, according to his wish, his ashes were buried on a remote moor near a property he had once owned in the north of Scotland.

Both a Canadian actor and a film director and noted for his 1920 screen adaptation of Robert Louis

Stevenson's *Dr Jekyll and Mr Hyde*, starring John Barrymore, **John Stuart Robertson** was born in 1878 in London, Ontario.

Married to the screen writer Josephine Lovett, he died in 1964, while he is the subject of *Old John Robertson* – a 1968 song by The Byrds.

Born in 1973 in Hamilton, Ontario, **Kathleen Robertson** is the Canadian actress and producer best known for her roles, from 1990 to 1993, in the sitcom *Manic Mansion* and, from 1994 to 1997, in the teen drama series *Beverley Hills, 90210*.

Also hailing from Ontario, **George R. Robertson**, born in 1933, is the actor best known for his roles in the *Police Academy* series of comedy films, while in 2004 he was the recipient of the Humanitarian Award at Canada's Gemini Awards.

Nominated for a Young Artist Award for her screen debut in the 2003 film *The Ghost Club*, Brittany Leanna Robertson is the American actress better known as **Britt Robertson**.

Born 1990 in Charlotte, North Carolina, her other film credits include the 2006 *Keeping Up with the Steins*, the 2011 *Scream 4* and, from 2013, *Delivery Man*.

Behind the camera lens, **Hugh A. Robertson**, born in 1932 in Brooklyn, New York, was the African-American film director and editor who won the BAFTA Award for Best Editing for his work on the 1969 *Midnight Cowboy*.

Also nominated for an Academy Award for Film Editing for his work on the film, he edited the 1971 *Shaft*; he died in 1988.

In the world of literature, **James Robertson**, born in 1958 and growing up in Bridge of Allan, Stirlingshire, is the acclaimed Scottish novelist whose *The Testament of Gideon Mack* was long-listed for the 2006 Man Booker Prize.

With other works that include *Joseph Knight*, *And the Land Lay Still* and *The Fanatic*, he also runs the independent publishing company *Kettillonia* in addition to being a co-founder of the Scots language imprint *Itchy Coo*, aimed at young people.

Bearers of the Robertson name have also excelled in the highly competitive world of sport.

In the rough and tumble that is the game of rugby union, **Bruce Robertson** is the New Zealand former player born in 1952.

Considered one of the best centres in New Zealand rugby union history, he played 34 tests with his national team the All Blacks between 1971 and 1982.

In the creative world of music, **Robbie Robertson** is the inductee of the Canadian Songwriters Hall of Fame ranked 59th in *Rolling Stone* magazine's list of the 100 Greatest Guitarists of all Time.

Born Jamie Robert Klegerman in Toronto in 1943, and taking the 'Robertson' surname from his stepfather, he is famed for his work as lead guitarist and main songwriter with The Band – composing classics that include *The Night They Drove Old Dixie Down*, *The Weight* and *Broken Arrow*.

The Band, who worked for a time on tour with Bob Dylan, are the subject of the 1978 Martin Scorsese film *The Last Waltz*.

In addition to having enjoyed a successful solo career with hit singles between 1979 and 1981 that include *Bang, Bang*, *Kool in the Kaftan* and *To Be or Not To Be*, Brian Alexander Robertson, better known as **B.A. Robertson**, has also penned hits for other artists.

Born in Glasgow in 1948, the musician, songwriter and actor wrote the Mike Rutherford hit *The Living Years* and also wrote or co-wrote the Cliff

Richard best-selling singles *Carrie*, *Hot Shot* and *Wired for Sound*.

As an actor, he played the lead role in the 1982 film *Living Apart Together*, while as a songwriter he also wrote *We Have a Dream* for the 1982 World Cup Scotland squad.

Two bearers of the name who left a decidedly tasty legacy for posterity were the Scottish grocer **James Robertson**, born in Paisley in 1831, and his wife **Marion**.

Operating in the early days from a small grocery shop in the town, the couple used Seville oranges to create what has become the famous international brand known as Robertson's "Golden Shred" marmalade, in addition to a range of fruit preserves.

James Robertson died in 1914 and was succeeded as company chairman by his eldest son John, while the Robertson's range of products has been owned since 2007 by Premier Foods.